ONLINE MEDIA INCLUDED
Audio Recordings
Printable Piano Accompaniments

Speed • Pitch • Balance • Loop

CONTENTS

Drummers' Delight (percussion trio w/piano) ....Edwards   2

High School Drummer (snare solo) ....Rackett   4

Mr. Boom-Boom (bass drum solo w/piano) ....Harr   6

Jumbo's Holiday (bass drum solo w/piano) ....Harr   7

Lexington (snare/bass duet)..Harr   8

Chesapeake (snare/bass duet) ....Harr   10

Newgulf Drummer (snare solo) ....Kelly   13

Yankee Doodle Fantasy (duet for snare/flute or picc) ....Rackett   14

American Patrol (snare solo w/piano; opt. fl/picc/clar) .....Meacham/Harr   18

Two of Us (snare duet) ....Buggert   20

Saratoga (snare/bass duet) ....Harr   22

Susquehanna (snare/bass duet) ....Harr   24

Thundering Through (snare solo) ....Buggert   27

Drummers' Canzonetta (snare trio) ....Buggert   28

To access recordings and PDF piano accompaniments, go to:
www.halleonard.com/mylibrary

Enter Code
6814-2606-9533-6016

ISBN 978-1-4950-7511-7

7777 W. BLUEMOUND RD. P.O. BOX 13819 MILWAUKEE, WI 53213

Visit Hal Leonard Online at
www.halleonard.com

T0056090

Drummers' Delight
Percussion Trio with Piano

Steve Edwards

00196893

High School Drummer

Snare Drum Solo

Arthur H. Rackett

00196893

6

Use two hard sticks and
play at or near the center
of the drum head.

Mr. Boom-Boom
Solo for Bass Drum and Piano

Solo Bass Drum

Haskell Harr

00196893

Jumbo's Holiday
Solo for Bass Drum and Piano

Use two hard sticks and play at or near the center of the drum head.

Solo Bass Drum

Haskell Harr

Lexington
Duet for Snare and Bass Drums

Haskell Harr

B.D. to be played with two hard sticks, at or near center of drum head.

TRIO

Chesapeake
Duet for Snare and Bass Drums

Haskell Harr

B.D to be played with two hard sticks, at or near center of drum head.

TRIO

This page intentionally blank

Newgulf Drummer

Snare Drum Solo

A.H. Kelly

Yankee Doodle Fantasy

Duet for Snare Drum and Flute or Piccolo

Flute/Piccolo

Arthur H. Rackett

5 Stands for **5** stroke roll from hand to hand
9 „   „   **9** „   „   „   „   „   „   „   „
11 „   „   **11** „   „   „   **Left** „ **Right only**

16

American Patrol
Snare Drum Solo with Piano
or Duet for Snare with Flute/Piccolo/Clarinet*

F.W. Meacham
Arranged by Haskell Harr

* Flute/Piccolo and Clarinet parts available for download (PDF) using the access code printed on page 1.

Two of Us
Snare Drum Duet

R.W. Buggert

00196893

Saratoga
Duet for Snare and Bass Drums

Haskell Harr

B.D to be played with two hard sticks, at or near center of drum head.

TRIO

Susquehanna
Duet for Snare and Bass Drums

Haskell Harr

B.D to be played with two hard sticks, at or near center of drum head.

00196893

TRIO   Snare part should be played on the rim (or softly on the drum) as background rhythm for the bass drum.

Thundering Through

Snare Drum Solo

R.W. Buggert

00196893

Drummers' Canzonetta
Snare Drum Trio*

R.W. Buggert

* For ease of page turning, this trio is also available for download (PDF) using the access code printed on page 1.

Music for Percussion from the

Rubank Educational Catalog

SNARE DRUM SOLOS Unaccompanied

HL04479337	Bobbin' Back (Buggert) *Grade 4*
HL04479340	Echoing Sticks (Buggert) *Grade 4*
HL04479345	Rolling Accents (Buggert) *Grade 4*

MARIMBA/XYLOPHONE SOLOS with Piano Accompaniment

HL04479361	Ave Maria (Schubert/arr. Edwards) *Grade 2*
HL04479367	Flight of the Bumblebee (Rimsky-Korsakov/arr. Quick) *Grade 4*
HL04479368	Hungarian Dance No. 5 (Brahms/arr. Quick) *Grade 3*
HL04479372	Largo from New World Symphony (Dvořák/arr. Quick) *Grade 2.5*
HL04479374	Light Cavalry Overture (von Suppe/arr. Quick) *Grade 4.5*
HL04479475	March Militaire, Op. 51 No. 1 (Schubert/arr. Quick) *Grade 3.5*
HL04471140	Music for Marimba, Vol. 1 (2- or 3-mallet solos/duets) (Jolliff) *Grade 1-2*
HL04471150	Music for Marimba, Vol. 2 (2- or 3-mallets) (Jolliff) *Grade 2-3*
HL04471160	Music for Marimba, Vol. 3 (3- or 4-mallets) (Jolliff) *Grade 3*
HL04479480	Rhapsodic Fantasie (Edwards/based on Liszt's *Hungarian Rhapsody No. 2*) *Grade 4*

DRUM ENSEMBLES Instrumentation as marked

HL04479349	Double Drummin' (two snares w/piano accompaniment) (Harr) *Grade 2*
HL04479351	Flinging It Threefold (trio for three snares) (Buggert) *Grade 2*
HL04479356	Ticonderoga (trio for two snares and bass) (Harr) *Grade 3*
HL04479359	We Three (trio for three snares) (Buggert) *Grade 3*